Voices from a Hidden Classroom

Versions of the following poems from Special Ed have appeared in:
Texas Observer: *Paulie's Bouncing Bible, Strange Tears*; The Progressive:
*No Tongue in Cheek, Innocent with Guilty Hands, Gloria's Dream Box, Paulie
and Sadie Play Catch, Checkers with Rats, Touch is a Broken Branch, Carlos*;
Red River Review: *Official Business*.

First Edition.
NYQ Books™ is an imprint of The New York Quarterly Foundation, Inc.

Library of Congress Control Number: 2012930601
ISBN: 978-1-935520-47-4

The New York Quarterly Foundation, Inc.
P. O. Box 2015
Old Chelsea Station
New York, NY 10113

www.nyqbooks.org

Set in Filosophia, New Century Schoolbook, Base 9, Interstate,
Quadraat Sans

Layout and Design: Warren Lehrer
Cover Design: Warren Lehrer www.earsay.org

SPECIAL Ed

Voices from a Hidden Classroom

poems by

Dennis J. Bernstein

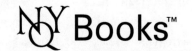

The New York Quarterly Foundation, Inc.
New York, New York

Preface

Known to many as a tireless, muckraking reporter, Dennis Bernstein, the host of several daily investigative programs on the Pacifica Radio Network for nearly three decades is at heart, and has been for over four decades—a poet. When I first met Dennis in the mid-seventies, he was working by day as a 'special ed' teacher in Far Rockaway, Queens. By night, early mornings, and weekends he was writing and studying poetry.

I watched him get drawn into investigative journalism, not by design or as a career plan, but out of necessity—to tell the truth about covert and under-reported wars, and the brutality, inequality, and corruption he found inside corporate and governmental hierarchies. By the late seventies, broadcast journalism took hold of Dennis and wouldn't let go. After all, he possessed the right stuff: a keen memory for details, an uncanny scent for going down dimly lit paths, an ability to connect dots like few can or do, a relentless penchant for asking questions others dare not (or don't even know to) ask, an eye for the story, a compassionate voice to tell it, and most often—knowing how to make room for others to tell their own stories.

But journalism requires precise answers, clear beginnings, middles, ends—facts. Poetry, at its best, Dennis Bernstein's poetry, sings in the territory of feelings, opposing images, multitudinous grays, dreams, whispers, the silences between thoughts, unspeakable fears and yearnings. All through the years, before and after broadcasting his daily clarion calls for justice, and doggedly chasing otherwise unpursued stories for drive time listeners (in the a.m. with Contra-Gate in New York, later in the p.m. with Flashpoints in the Bay Area), Dennis quietly practiced the life-sustaining craft of his poetry.

Some of Dennis'earliest poems were published in the *New York Quarterly*, starting in 1975 with "Getting Tough" a street-smart, death-threat poem which William Packard published again a few years later in NYQ's *Best Of* Anthology, and discussed in his *Writer's Craft* feature on Dennis. With the encouragement and mentoring of the late poet, biographer, and activist Muriel Rukeyser, Dennis became a voracious reader (and champion) of other people's poetry. Inspired by the work and life of his teacher, he founded the Muriel Rukeyser Center for the Arts in Brooklyn, and produced the Muriel Rukeyser reading series for WBAI, airing interviews with Rukeyser, Robert Bly, Grace Paley, Denise Levertov, Audre Lorde, Quincy Troupe, and Gregory Orr. And he recorded and aired most of William Packard's plays, including the mini-masterpiece, "Ty Cobb."

It's fitting that the *New York Quarterly*—started by Packard—is publishing Dennis Bernstein's debut book of poetry—the first in a series of DB collections to illuminate their way into volumes (of prison poems, pizza joint poems, family poems, radio poems). *Special Ed* grows out of his years teaching "troubled" middle schoolers on the eastern most edge of Queens. Many of these poems first took form back in the seventies, and have since been revisited—pruned, put aside, and re-written—as part of Dennis' long-term love-wrestle with words, punctuation, line breaks, and erasers. Some of these poems were written more recently, with the help of vivid memories, not only of his years as a teacher but as a rough-hewn, special ed kid himself, more versed, at that time, in gymnastics and boxing then the three Rs.

Dennis knew how to reach his students, many of whom were in his class because his colleagues had given them up as 'unteachable,' if not wired for a life of criminality. I remember Dennis proudly reading his students prose poems to me, written from the vantage point of Mr. PinDrop, an imaginary character who lived within them and could hear and see things nobody else could. The PinDrop poems could go on for pages. Many were filled with misspellings and grammatical errors, but they were tough, tender, shockingly-revealing, and often funny. Somehow, in Mr. Bernstein's class, these 'illiterate' kids couldn't stop writing.

In these short, sharp, soulful poems, Dennis Bernstein opens wide the door to the inside of the inside of his classroom. Tina, Paulie, JoJo, Gloria, Pierre, Marilyn—a cast of dozens—are in attendance, reporting the news, making art, listening for pin drops.

Warren Lehrer
AUTHOR/ARTIST

I was an undiagnosed dyslexic until age 22. In the first grade, I was called a "retard" by classmates, egged on by a teacher who called me "damaged goods" and "naturally stupid." This teacher requested a meeting with my mother to deliver good and bad news. The bad news was that I was "borderline mentally retarded." The good news was that with the support of tutors and a special school, I could lead a perfectly normal life, get married, have a job, and even a couple of kids.

My teacher presented the evidence to my mother in the form of penmanship papers, which she claimed demonstrated my inability to grasp even the most basic concepts of learning. "Look here," she said, presenting her evidence Exhibit A: a worksheet of W's that turned into flying M's. The pages were covered with the letters—on the lines, between the lines, outside the margins, and flying off of the page in all directions.

My mother turned to me and asked if I understood the difference between a W and an M. "Yes," I said, "they are cousins having fun flying together." My mother had five sisters and two brothers and I had an army of cousins.

While I understood the basic concept of writing on the line, when it came to distinguishing the difference between a W and an M, I ran into problems. The letters played tricks on my eyes. W's became M's and vice versa, and often I could not tell the difference. "Make" became "wake" and "war" flipped into "mar." So many of the 26 letters would shapeshift before my eyes. Numbers were a nightmare as well. 3's became E's and "10" turned into "to." I ended up adding numbers and letters to come up with fantastic equations like $Z + Z = 33$.

When I was growing up, there was no such thing as Special Education. I was often sent next door to a reading class a grade below mine, where the younger kids left me in the dust of my own stutters.

When asked to read aloud, I stumbled along haltingly, word by word, like a hiker taking a steep incline barefooted, falling many times. I rarely finished the assigned paragraph, the teacher chided me for being lazy or not paying attention and the snickers of my classmates cut to the bone.

I was lost until the fourth grade when a teacher saw my struggle and accepted it as her challenge. Mrs. Edwards, a seasoned teacher a few years away from retirement caught on early in the year. She gave the class an assignment to write a story about what our desks say to each other at night when we are gone. I thought the assignment was so funny and intriguing! I went home and wrote for hours. I even skipped Superman and my other TV favorites to fill the pages of my notebook with talking desks. I could hardly wait to read my story.

The next day, when asked to read it, I also could hardly read a word of what I had written. After a struggle, stuttering and stumbling over words that were changing shape and floating over the sides of the page, Mrs. Edwards showed mercy and asked me to read the rest to her later so others could have a chance to share their work.

When we met later, Mrs. Edwards didn't ask me to *read* my story, but rather, she asked me to *tell* her my story. I told her that the desks got headaches when kids slammed books on them and how it reeked and made them want to barf when students forgot leftover egg salad and salami and cheese sandwiches inside them to rot.

As I spoke, she wrote, then typed, and then handed me my story, my first byline: "Talking Desks" by Dennis Bernstein.

She then asked me to read her my story from the typed pages. I stumbled, but not nearly as much as before, and by the second time through, I could read my own words with very little trouble. This was the first time a teacher had given me a chance to show that I knew how to read.

During that year, Mrs. Edwards also helped me discover that what I lacked in reading skills, I more than made up for with excellent oratory skills and a finely tuned memory. I was appointed the student tour guide for a traveling exhibition of copies of masterpieces from the Museum of Modern Art, leading students to each piece and describing the art from a memorized script. I starred in the class play, as Columbus discovering that the world was round. For each of these projects, Mrs. Edwards read me my lines, then I would read and memorize them myself from the page.

One day, Mrs. Edwards held a special recess in the gym. There in the center of the high-ceilinged gym was the first trampoline I had seen. After seeing what it could do, I was ecstatic: A great big bed with springs around the outside instead of hidden inside. I had already broken several of my mother's beds, bouncing on them, and once even broke my head open "Superman-ning" off the bed into a steel radiator.

The class gathered around the trampoline and one at a time, we mounted it. When my turn came, I climbed onto the bouncing machine and bounced into a new reality. I felt free—freed from my earthbound skin, my pain, and my fears. I bounced and reached for the ceiling. When it was time to dismount, I refused to come down. I had already left the room, flown the coop of the restrictive school day and had joined the birds that had long ago flown off the side of the page of my penmanship pages in the first grade.

Finally, Mrs. Edwards yelled at me to get down and give someone else a chance, but I just kept bouncing. Eventually the gym teacher heard the fuss and mounted the trampoline, put a firm hand on my shoulder, and ended my first flight.

Later, Mrs. Edwards asked why I refused to get down. She wasn't *angry*. She was *curious*. I shrugged and said I didn't know. Of course, I was unable to explain it then, but what Mrs. Edwards honed in on was that I had found something that I really loved to do, and she needed to figure out a way to make it a part of my educational process. Soon thereafter, she arranged weekly gymnastics classes for me with the gym teacher, who happened to be an accomplished gymnast. Needless to say, I learned quickly.

While learning in the classroom by traditional means was a daily chore, my success in gymnastics was astounding. The more complicated the trick, the more it required me to visualize the move, and then put my body where my mind was. Slowly, I was able to apply this process of visualization—body learning—to the formal learning process and it changed everything. I learned to read diagrams, that illustrated how the body needed to move to make a new trick, and read stories about the latest stars on the gymnastics scene.

The bottom line: This single teacher, Mrs. Edwards, who had compassion, who found my strength, and used it to work through my weaknesses, found a way for me to feel success and participate in my education.

This is not to say that gymnastics was a solution to all of my learning problems. Indeed, as a junior in high school I won the New York State High School Trampoline Championship and was the YMCA Trampoline Champion for the state, but I was left back for failing algebra, biology and mechanical drawing. The fact that I was still an undiagnosed dyslexic in desperate need of a pair of glasses guaranteed me a bumpy ride all the way through high school.

Helped by the devoted tutoring of several aunts, who were all New York City public school teachers, and a cheerleading section lead by my mom, I made it through high school, college, and even got a Master's degree.

I became a teacher of special students, so-called emotionally disturbed kids. Most of them were rightfully troubled; hungry, frightened, and abused. The poems in this book come from my own experiences as a special student and from those of the kids I taught in Far Rockaway and the South Bronx.

I welcome you to the world of *Special Ed: Voices from a Hidden Classroom* and invite you inside to meet the kids I taught. These are the kids I struggled to keep awake days, who thirty years later still sit in a classroom in the back of my mind. They've kept me awake nights—raising their hands to be heard.

Dennis J. Bernstein

ROLL CALL

*For J-Ha, the Late George M and Dorothy Pfeffer Bernstein,
and my brother, Robert Alan Bernstein and family.*

Tina delivers the morning news.
Facts are artfully stacked,
but rarely exaggerated—Tragedy
is a popular theme. Today T.J. Harris
makes Tina's headlines: *"His mom
jammed a hatpin through his pop's heart
after the old man clocked her.
Cops kept the hatpin for evidence."*

Pierre's on the run from Haiti.
He had to leave in a hurry
when the soldiers came to cut
his mother's tongue out.
He says they took her tongue
because she talked too much.
But Pierre could never get enough;
even when she scolded him, it was kisses.
Some nights he dreams about his mother's
tongue, flies it around like a magic carpet.

SILENT PARTNER

Our classroom is the only one with curtains.
Gloria and Marilyn pieced them together
and sewed up their own friendship at the same time.
It was the first day of school. Marilyn fluttered around
in two languages. Gloria never uttered a word—
she just listened with her entire body.
Together they cut and stitched and sewed all morning
with the strong thread of first beginnings.

PAULIE'S BOUNCING BIBLE

He carried his basketball wherever he went.
Sometimes he bounced it fiercely
and took aim at hoops
that only he could see.
Sometimes he twirled it
on one finger
like a bulbous ballerina.
But mostly Paulie
held the ball
between his palms,
against his chest,
the way a preacher holds a bible
to make god's point.
Just like his mother's little Christ,
it strengthened his grip on things,
extended his palms around a world
he was barely able to hold onto.

TAMISHA'S ALPHABET

Tamisha makes up her own words.
Her alphabet is full of sounds
that come before A and after Z—
The 26 letters in between
only get in her way.

ONE-BOY BAND

Richard hates math, but he's a master of mouth noise.
He can click and clack and pop and whistle—
he's mastered pitch and attack with the skill
of a seasoned jazz man. He's a one-boy band:
plays a dozen different instruments
between his lips and his hands.
Late nights, he sips deeply from Pop's vinyl—
Coltrane, Mingus, Lady Day and Miles—
His father chants these names as he falls asleep,
blue notes mingling with thunder and sirens.

KITCHEN MAGIC

Manny says his mom is a magician.
Every morning she pulls breakfast
out of a hat. At dinner time,
with nothing up her sleeves,
or in her pocketbook,
she waves a magic wand
and a big bowl of soup appears.

SCHOOL OF MUSIC AND ART

Freddie plays the guitar with a hammer,
after Jason jerks it out of his hands and uses it
as a laser gun against invading martians.
I am amazed to see how many pieces the guitar is in
after Freddie plays his blues. We glue the pieces
into a fine work of abstract art
and hang it on the wall.

PEA-BRAIN

"This one's a real pea-brain."
That's what Dean Riley tells me
as he shoves Jason into my classroom
and shuts the door in our faces.
Next morning, Jason is spinning jacks
on the hard-tile floor. He calls me over
and insists I hunker down for a front-row seat.
"Look," says Jason,
"look at the ballerinas dancing on their tiptoes."

HEROES AND SAINTS

The State Home for the Aging is a forgotten Island of loss,

just down the block, and around the corner from our schoolhouse.

It's ringed in by a twelve-foot-high barbed-wire fence, meant to

keep out the junkies who use flashlights to search for their veins

after sunset. On one side of the home is a hospital and across the

street, a torched-out funeral parlor. The sun never comes to the

residents of the old-age home, except as reflected through the

eyes of my kids.

PAULIE AND SADIE PLAY CATCH

Paulie is playing with Sadie
at the old-age home. Paulie
takes out his pink high-bouncer
and places it firmly into Sadie's hands.
He whispers for her to roll him the ball.
Sadie smiles like a toothless child
when Paulie takes this stance—
poised to catch her fading world.
For Sadie, Paulie is a patron saint,
no matter how many days of the week
he gets cuffed to a wall in juvenile hall.

CHARITY WORK

At one hundred and three, Carrie Blaustein is
convinced she is doing something good for humanity.
She is stuffing and stacking Goodwill envelopes
that are not there. Richard, who can't count past
five, is keeping track of Carrie's growing numbers,
stacking piles of twenty per her instructions—
Richard accompanies their collaboration with his
own whistled version of "My Favorite Things."

THE WAY IT IS

Some days, I can hold back their hunger

with a recipe for sweet potato pie,

or divert it with a story about the biggest lie ever told.

Sometimes, I can snip the fuse from the dynamite

and close the charge before it explodes.

I can rescue them from the murder scene

with songs or poetry or an urgent session

on the trampoline.

Other days, death combs its hair

with the bones of my children. . .

INNOCENT WITH GUILTY HANDS

Karen says her hands
have a mind of their own.
They come and go as they please.
They take long walks
and break off violently
in her dreams.
They pinch and slap
and steal and scheme.
They crave the feel
of matches against gasoline.

The black bitch cat scratches what's left of the
rat's brain clean from the gray half-moon of its skull.
A few feet away Jojo plays with a red pick-up truck
his mind is driving to a country called California,
where his mother serves french fries to red-and-
white-faced surfers.

The cat finishes up lunch and starts rough-tonguing
his raggedy paws. The white sun burns an eye into
noon. Jojo feels the heat bearing down on the crown
of his head, like a hand, like the barber's sweaty palm
pressing him into stillness to avoid drawing blood.

Jojo is thinking about his tenth birthday. He is
studying his ten fingers, thinking of each one as a
year. He can taste the hunger that still drives the
cat's tongue into the rat's bony skull.

He wants some of those french fries his mother is
serving. He's thinking maybe of heading out west
to do some surfing himself, and kick back for some
tasty eats with mom.

RERUNS

T.J.'s been having trouble sleeping
ever since his mom plunged the hatpin
into his pop's chest.
He hears voices when he goes to bed,
and watches reruns on a tiny screen
in the back of his head.

God offered Gloria a chunk of chocolate and a silver dollar
for a smile. But Gloria said "oh no" to god, "no es posible."
Okay, said god, Okay. How about the finest house on a
hill in heaven with a hundred angels singing sweetly
and a basket of green apples the size of full moons—
for just one smile?

"No, No, de ningún modo," Gloria replied, and dreamt the
moon was spilling over with songs her mama sang as she
fell asleep and flew across the sky on a trapeze of high
notes. Ok, ok, said God, you drive a hard bargain; Here's
my final offer. I'll set your mama free and put the sunrise
back into your papa's eyes—for just one smile.

To this Gloria finally said "Si, Si, esta bien," her lips
easing up into a softening grin, her eyes glistening like
the dew on the early morning grass in front of the farm
house in Guatemala, after her mama was snatched up
by the soldiers for not telling them about the friendly
men who were living in the barn and helping plow
and seed our fields.

FELONY BOUNCING

Bobo was busted for breaking and entering.
He broke into school through a backdoor
in the boy's gym.
They caught him bouncing
bare-footed on the trampoline—just Bobo,
eyes closed, reaching for new heights.

GRAVITY LESSON

Cops cornered Terrence
and tossed him against the fence.
He cursed their mothers
when they cuffed him to a swing-set.
"I ain't done shit," he insisted.
"I just pushed the sucker over:
It was Gravity that broke his neck."

ACCOMPLICE

Regina sells nickel bags.
She does a brisk business before class.
She stashes the cash in secret pockets
stitched to the insides of her pants.

If she comes to class, poetry is her calling.
If I call the cops, she'll be scribing
her poems on prison walls.

OUTSIDE THE HOCK SHOP

Paulie found a gold band in the gutter.
It took two cops to pry it out of his fist.
"It's mine," Paulie protested, *"possession
is nine-tenths of the law."*
Cops said the tenth part was never his to own.

PIOUS UNCLE PHILLY

Every fall Jason's Great Uncle Philly spends ten days
trying to paste the leaves back onto his maple tree.
Folks on the block say Philly's gone crazy.
Freddie says some nazi-kraut shot out his lights.
Father Sal at St. Paul the Pious says it's all a bunch of bull
Pasting back god's leaves is just Philly's way of praying.

RECIPES FOR READING

They are happiest
when they are eating,
so I teach by feeding them.
We speed-read the recipes
and do the math. Our
classroom chemistry
rarely lets us down.
Today Jason wants to know
how many calories
in a three-syllable word?

ONE PEA AT A TIME

Tracy's always hungry and he's always trying to hide it.
He's ashamed of this gnawing at the center that makes
him tremble and flicker like a pinball machine.
Sometimes he keeps his chin tucked in so tightly,
it looks like it's fastened to his chest with a safety pin.
Some days he's too proud to be fed. Right now,
he's drowning green peas in chocolate pudding,
and rescuing them with a plastic fork, one pea at a time.

NO SPILLED MILK

Ricardo can't spell the word spell for beans,
but he knows how to tell me
he's hungry in three languages.
Today his eyes are blinking maydays
from a ship lost at sea. It is only eight-thirty
and he's sure he hears the lunch ladies
with their brash laughter and purple hair.
Ricardo salivates. Lunch is a mirage. By snack break
he is shaking so hard he needs to hold his milk
carton with both hands to keep from spilling it.

MIDNIGHT SHOPPING

I didn't break the law, Paulie says.
I followed god's orders.
Mom was hungry and Jesus said
to feed the poor.
So I went to the grocery store
and gathered up a nice Christmas feast
for me and mom.

The temperature rises. A fist of twelve-year-olds corner a chunky rat and beat it into a puddle of ooze and cracked bone. After they've had enough of the beast, they turn their frenzy on themselves. They chain-smoke stolen packs of Camels and practice their curses. At high noon, they trap a stray calico and hang the cat by its tail. They pelt it with rocks launched from home-made sling-shots. Cheap wine pumps up the ferocity of the attack. When it comes time to move on, Terrence takes out his pop's pistol and puts a swift end to the cat's misery.

TALL TALE

Jason's Uncle Terrel
is too tall for basketball;
He has to bend down to dunk.
His wife climbs a step-ladder
to kiss him goodnight.
When he walks to work,
he bumps his head on the clouds.
When it rains, he's always
the first one to get wet.

BREAKFAST FIXINGS

Freddie found a perfect loaf of bread today.
Somebody left it on top of the payphone
downtown. Not a crumb out of place.
A good-looking loaf, ready for toast and jam,
perfect to cozy up with a couple of eggs
Freddie stole out of Dave's dairy case,
while the old man had his eyes trained
on a couple of jumpy kids,
hollering nickel and dime orders
for red string licorice.

PAINT CHIPS FOR THE QUEEN

Paint Chips on May-Day.
She tastes them on her lips,
long after she's finished
her corn flakes: Well past noon,
and her head is still bobbing
from her morning cereal.
She faints dramatically,
our Maypole Queen,
and lands in an ambulance
struggling to conjure the lines
of her acceptance speech
as the new Queen of May.

TRACY GOES FISHING

Tracy stands at the rim of the garbage bin
fishing for half-eaten peanut butter and jelly sandwiches
and fresh fruit. He dips and eats as fast as he can
before the blue-haired lunch ladies can wrestle
the fresh pickings out of his hands.
Tracy doesn't give a damn
about some invisible germs. He figures he'll die
faster from hunger than from a bunch
of tiny critters crawling around his insides.

SLAMMING THE DOOR ON CHRISTMAS

There's about fifty minutes left until Christmas recess. We are
heading for the gym. That's when Kiki calls out to Luce in Miss
Klein's class, just as we're passing by in the hallway. Miss Klein
slams shut the door while two of Kiki's fingers are still in the
door-jam. Her flesh is crushed easily between sharpened
edges of oak and steel.

The door is locked. I am banging on the window, vying for the
teacher's attention. Kiki is jumping up and down, crying for me
or god or her mother or someone to help her. I smash my fist
through the door-window and unlock it with a hand full of glass.
I am standing there with my arms around Kiki, surrounded by
screaming kids, both of us bleeding into the shards.

SLIPPERY SLOPE

January 1st. The new year is an old story
for Paulie. The same treacherous holes
in the calendar. Paulie rides his bike
down another slippery slope,
edges of ice threaten to flatten his tires.
Far as Paulie knows, Christmas is a broken promise—
Jesus never keeps his word.

WINTER FIRES

The flames always burn closer to the poor. "We can freeze to death or die from faulty heaters," says Jason's Uncle Jojo. In this part of the city, shoddy summer shacks become lethal tinder—they begin to flare up in November, and the smoke doesn't clear until early spring. Sometimes it's hard to tell what's really burning. "Hey Freddie," Tina yells, "isn't that your house with the broken-down chimney and the jacked-up Caddy out front?"

STRANGE TEARS

Paulie finds tears
in the oddest places.

He finds them
in the mirror's eyes.

He knows they can't be his.
He's too tough.

Tina says the body count was up to ten
when she stopped by the fire on the way to school.
At noon, the flames were still kicking up clouds.
"They carried them out on stretchers," Tina says,
"white sheets pulled up over their heads."
Everyone knew when Pops Mahoney came through—
his big belly was puffed up
like the last Parachute at Coney Island.

MARKSMAN OF SORTS

Jason's Uncle Stax
is a phlegm-throwing
semi-automatic; Stax
can spit the whistle
out of a cop's lips
in the middle of a
rush-hour drive-by.

THE DREAMERS

Sometimes I can see them leaving,

disappearing even as they sit before me.

Some teachers like to punish them for leaving,

enjoy catching them in the act of departure—

yanking them back by their names.

I let them dream.

Sometimes I read about their journeys

in journals that no one knows they keep.

GLORIA'S DREAM BOX

I keep my dreams
in a dream box under the bed.

My sister Carmen says
it's just an empty box.

Carmen never sees what I see.

Her eyes are dark
like a night without stars.

Jason blamed yesterday's fire
on an infestation of fireflies.
He says they hide in the floor boards
                              and flare up—
Where there's flies there's always fire.

PHONICS

Richard finds a stick of dynamite under the boardwalk.
He is unable to read its faded label. He couldn't read it
if it was in bold print and hot off the press. He thinks
it's a Roman Candle that fell through the cracks last
4th of July. He scrapes it with a pocket knife, strikes it
against rock, but nothing happens. Tonight on the beach,
as an army of street preachers start setting fires to stay
high and warm, when no one's paying Richard much mind—
he'll just flip his "flare" into the flames and test out
the unread powers of his new find.

FLYING MACHINES

Richard is as hyper as a hummingbird,
except when he gets to swinging.
Then he can linger for hours,
steady as a heart beat. Sometimes
he sneaks out in the middle of the night
and swings himself to the stars. For hours,
he aims his toes skyward, the slender
arrow of his body, soaring and dipping—
transformed into a dozen different
flying machines, then one glorious eagle.

MASKING FOR TOUCH

They are making masks out of papier mâché.

One lies down, the other does the sculpting;

the toughest kids take turns touching—

tracing highways around cheekbones and chins,

around the crucial hairpin switches

of nostrils and lips. For a moment, touch

is more than a threat crushed into a fist—

It's the river of their ancestors

as it flows through their veins.

Soon, a fragile new face is lifted,

born with a life of its own,

and lightning is breaking across

the dark eyes of its creator.

WHEN TINA'S FULL MOON HOWLS

Tina loves to paint the night.
Her skies are always militant
with bobcats bounding and black
snakes rearing back—fangs up
against the rest of the world.
When Tina's full moon howls,
the wolves of the world join in.

DIAMONDS OF ANGER

Freddie can get into a brawl with an empty room.
Today he shatters glass to make his point.
Everybody laughs when Freddie lashes out,
except for Marilyn—she sees diamonds
in Freddie's broken glass. She gathers up the pieces
and glues them into rings, broaches and bracelets
for every girl in the class.

WHEN TOUCH BREAKS A BRANCH

Touch is high voltage for Tanya.
Today she shook and sweat
right where she stood
when Pablo put his arm around her.
She twitched and tilted her head
until her ear was touching her shoulder blade.
Her neck was so bent out of shape
it looked like a broken branch.

PRESENT TENSE

Can anyone give me a sentence
using the present tense for "remember"?

Jojo?

I remember the look on Fat-Jake's face
after my sister shot him.

SHOPPING FOR GHOSTS

"Mrs. Jonetta James was taken away
to the crazy house today," says Tina.
"They came and spun her up like a mummy
and sped away with the bubble flashing.
Her boy Tiny died of 'cute' leukemia,
but Mrs. James kept dropping him off
and picking him up from school."

OUTSIDE AGITATOR IS MISSING

Sometimes Paulie likes to come to class
without coming to school.
He stands outside the classroom window,
weighing in with his opinions
when he has something relevant to say.

KILLER SOUP

I dream Richard is drowning
in a giant bowl of alphabet soup.
Teachers around the edges
keep throwing him O's
and other letters of rescue
which fall just out of reach.

OFFICIAL BUSINESS

The desk cop
at the first precinct
says Bobo's Aunt Bell
is a barrel of angry bitches
in one skinny body. He says
Bell socked a cop last night,
and obstructed official police business.
Bell says the cop she clocked
had no damn business
officially grabbing her ass.

FREDDY-BOY

Throwing stones through the moon.
Hurling stares at passing strangers.
Breaking stars into the windows
of a torched-out tenement
on 60th Street, under the El,
between the rumble
of the subway and the sea.

BRUCE LEE GET LOST

Sara sews her pencils to her shirt-sleeves.
She's tired of having them swiped
and hacked in two,
by karate-chopping boy-wonders,
who want her to think
they are meaner than Bruce Lee
and Batman in one bad-ass body.

SMALL MIRACLE

Tina and Regina are poised for battle.
They've been at it since the early bell.
Last clash left them both bloody
and anxious for revenge.
Jason predicts armed conflict by lunchtime.
But at a minute to noon, Richard strikes up
his one-boy band
with a new tune from the Jackson Five,
and the whole class breaks into dance—
A miracle of song will soothe their wounds
and quiet down the jittery angels of vengeance.

WHEN MARILYN STAYS HOME

This world is much too much for Gloria to bear.
She's always searching for a door in the day
to escape through. Marilyn's easy laughter
softens Gloria's way. But the sun never rises
when Marilyn stays home or plays hooky
under the boardwalk.

CLOSET MAN

Tracy could give you the shirt off his back, and he'd still be wearing three or four more. In class, they call him Closet-Man. He wears all his clothes because he never knows where he'll rest his head, once the light goes thin and night comes back to bite him.

THREE BIRDS WITH ONE STONE

"The other day, two gang-guys threatened to drop Paulie off the roof of the projects at 59th street. They had him hanging by the heels," according to Tina's account. "They said they'd drop him six floors if he didn't come up with some cash for them. Paulie wasn't scared. He laughed at them. He said, if god wanted him to die now, they might as well drop him and be done with it, and god will deal with them later. They pulled him up and slapped him around a little and then they let him go."

TYRONE'S EYES

Tyrone would never beat Tina with his hands or tie
her down. He took Tina with his eyes, sprang silent as a cat
on fresh snow: He leapt across rooms at her, caught her with
her pants down on the toilet-bowl or waking out of dreams.
He never said a word about it, never laid a finger on her.

CHECKERS WITH RATS

Jojo cries in his dreams.
Every night he's caught in the crossfire;
He's pummeled or cut or blasted
backwards at close range.
Jojo would rather stay up nights
and play checkers with rats,
than be shot at, or knifed,
as soon as he closes his eyes.

SCORPIO RISING

Tracy points to the scars all over his stomach and arms.
Little red stars, he calls them. This one, he says,
pointing to a fresh scar at the base of his wrist—that looks
like a spider with its torso missing—is Scorpio Rising.

WHAT BOBO KNOWS

The more the whiskey makes the rounds
the riskier the game gets.
His father hasn't made a hand
since the dealer broke the deck.
But now he's dealt a flush in spades.
Bobo feels the winner's rush.
He's ready for a celebration, but
the old man doesn't see the hand;
He's too damn drunk to see.

Bobo wants to call the win
and haul in the cash.
But does he dare?
He knows about the pistol
tucked in Tito's sock,
about the switch-blade Six-Pack
keeps up his sleeve
for some quick magic:
Bobo knows there are no sidekicks
or eye-winks, and no junior partners
when it comes to high-stakes poker
at Sticky's "Club" behind the projects
on a sweltering Friday night.

WHERE THE MUSIC BEGINS

Richard hates math but he counts on keeping time.
Today he found a stethoscope behind the hospital
and brought it to school for show and tell.
He put it up to his ears and against his chest,
began to snap his fingers to the beat of his own heart.
"This," he told us, *"is where the music begins."*

CARLOS

always prints his name
in capitals. It helps him feel
a little bigger in the world.

STAGE PRESENCE

It's five minutes before show time and Regina is M.I.A.
I search the hallways and the stairwells. I find her in
the girl's gym, right behind the auditorium. She is alone,
facing the corner. The smell of reefer is in the air. She
is rehearsing the poems she is about to recite;
I retreat and leave it to fate.

Now both cameras zoom in as Regina arrives on set seconds
before show time, exuding the confdence of a seasoned
performer. She takes her place center stage. The curtain
lifts to applause. Regina stands tall in the spotlight. Back
straight, chin up, head held high, she begins to recite
Langston Hughes: altering the words to suit her gender:
*I, Too, Sing America / I am the darker sister / They send me
to eat in the kitchen / when company comes / But
I laugh / And eat well / And grow strong. . .*

Regina evaporates into stage light and glitter. One
strong voice rises. All eyes upon her, she becomes the poet
and boldly speaks the truth of the poem as her own. She
is greeted by waves of applause that break the silence
and shake the stage where Regina stands, glowing
like a Georgia sun—

THE GREAT ESCAPE

Tony-boy searches the sand
for a sea-worthy shell.
He's poised to shrink down,
and sail to some unknown port
where the streets are not so hot
and the money grows on trees.

Acknowledgements

I want to thank Warren Lehrer for the heartfelt and long-term support of my work, for his editing and design, and for his incredible patience and guidance in bringing *Special Ed* into print. His faith in my work has been instrumental in my keeping it going in the face of all hurdles. Big thank you to Raymond Hammond for his mammoth efforts in keeping the *New York Quarterly* going, in the spirit of its founding editor, the late William Packard, and for his support in making *Special Ed* a reality. Huge embrace and thank you, to my partner, J-Ha Hasegawa, for love and support through all things. Great gratitude to cousins Ellen and David Conford, for literary support, their great friendship, in times of great need. And of course thank you goes out to my deceased father and mother, George M Bernstein, and Dorothy Pffefer Bernstein, for loving me to the limit, and supporting my work, without doubt or question.

Dennis J. Bernstein lives in San Francisco and has been a long-time front line reporter specializing in human rights and international affairs. He worked as associate editor with the Pacific News Service, and is currently the host/producer of "Flashpoints," a daily news magazine syndicated on Pacifica Radio. He is the recipient of many awards for his investigative reporting, including the Jessie Meriton White Sevice Award in International Journalism, The Art of Peace award, the American-Arab Anti-Discrimination reporting award, Media Alliance/Media Bash Investigative Reporting award, and his investigative reports have been recognized by Project Censored many times. In 2009, Pulse Media named him one of the "20 Top Global Media Figures."

Bernstein's articles and essays have appeared in numerous newspapers and magazines from the *New York Times*, *San Francisco Chronicle*, the *Nation*, and *Spin Magazine*, to *Kyoto Journal*, *Der Spiegel*, and *International Herald Tribune*. Bernstein is he author of *Henry Hyde's Moral Universe*, the co-author of two decks of political trading cards, *Friendly Dictators* and the *S&L Scandal Trading Cards*; his artist book/plays, *French Fries* and *GRRRHHHH!* co-authored with Warren Lehrer, are in the collections of the Museum of Modern Art, the Georges Pompidou Centre, and other museums around the world.

After earning a master's degree in Education, Bernstein taught Special Ed for ten years in schools and maxium security prisons. He has taught teens in the South Bronx and Brooklyn—how to report and produce for print and radio—and is the founder of the South Bronx Media Collective and Young Writers Radio Collective.

Bernstein started in radio as a poetry producer, and founded the Muriel Rukeyser Reading Series in Park Slope Brooklyn, and broadcast over WBAI, in New York City; the series was named after his teacher, the late poet and biographer, Muriel Rukeyser. Bernstein also produced the first complete live, 35 hour broadcast of James Joyce's *Ulysses* in the U.S. at New York's Bloomsday Bookstore and over Pacifica radio. His first poems appeared as a chapbook, *Particles of Light*, with woodcuts by Stan Kaplan. Bernstein's poetry has also been published widely in the *Texas Observer*, *New York Quarterly*, *The Progressive*, *ZYZZYVA*, *Bat City Review*, *The Poetry Super Highway* Poet of the Week, *Your Daily Poem*, *Red River Review*, *The Bird's Eye Review*, *J Journal*, *Helicon Nine*, *The Dickens*, *Dark Horse*, *Chimaera*, *Science for the People*, *Ars Medica*, and *The Bijou Review*.

CPSIA information can be obtained at www.ICGtesting.com
Printed in the USA
LVOW111058200412

278406LV00005B/2/P